This book is dedicated to my daughter and husband.

Thank you for doing all the farm chores so I could create this book.

I'm so lucky to have you.

Thank you to my friend Brittany for being the first person to ever purchase one of my doodles.

Finally, I appreciate my friend Ph-
Oebe who provided me a space that al-
Lowed me to work quic-
Kly, quiet-
Ly and pr-
Ovided f-
Ree coffe-
E and fizzy water.

D1096447

ISBN: 9798731977982
Printed by 217 Digital in the United States of America.

For more content, visit
https://www.teacherspayteachers.com/Store/217-Digital

Letter A Objects

Letter B Objects

Letter C Objects

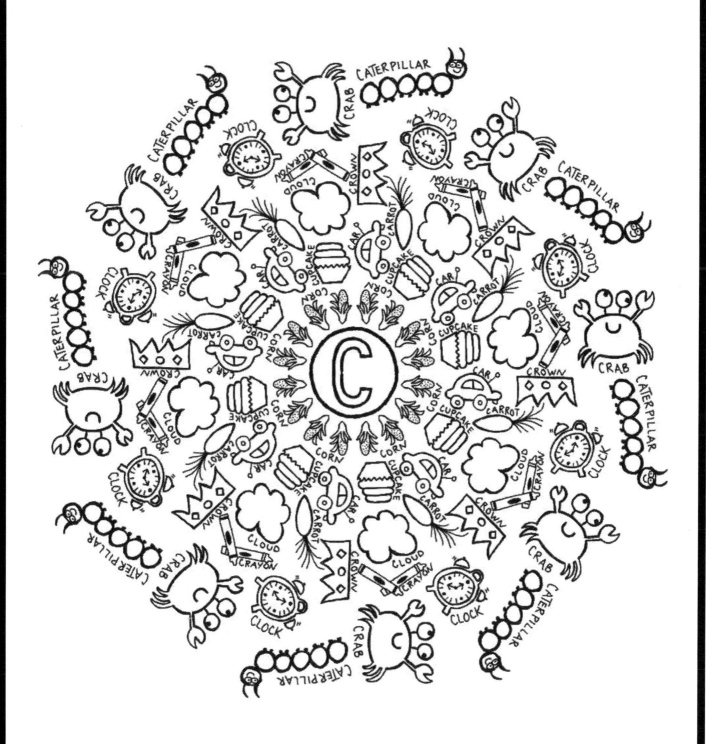

Letter D Objects

Letter E Objects

Letter F Objects

Letter G Objects

Letter H Objects

Letter I Objects

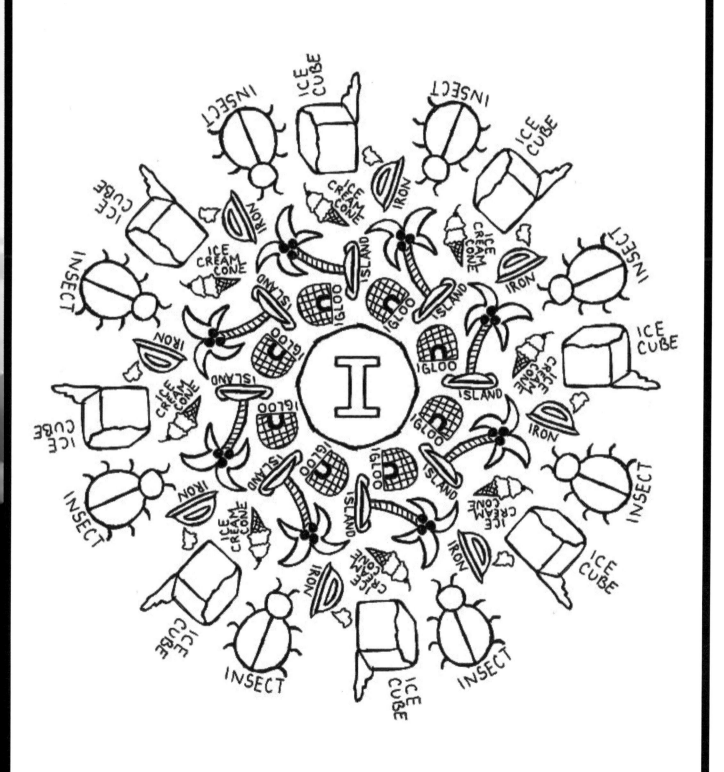

Letter J Objects

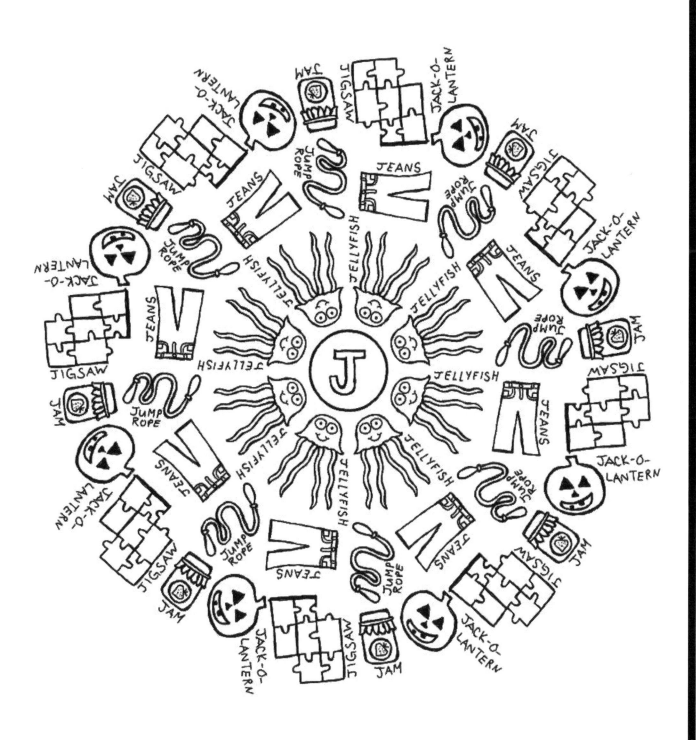

Letter K Objects

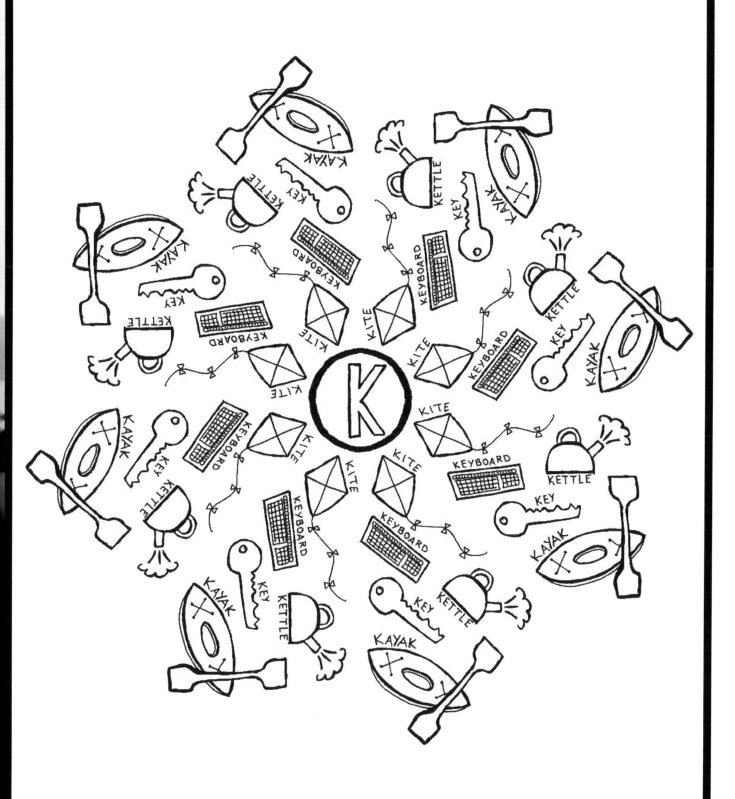

Letter L Objects

Letter M Objects

Letter N Objects

Letter O Objects

Letter P Objects

Letter Q Objects

Letter R Objects

Letter S Objects

Letter T Objects

Letter U Objects

Letter V Objects

Letter W Objects

Letter X Objects

Letter Y Objects

Letter Z Objects

Made in the USA
Middletown, DE
07 July 2022

68603632R00031